KIRKLEES LIBRARIES
MUSEUMS & ARTS

ACC. NO. 250 039 530
CLASS 780.91
DEPT. WK   CHECKED

KU-016-465

It's Easy To Play Children's Songs.

K Kirklees
Leisure
Services

Libraries, Museums & Arts Division,
Red Doles Lane,
Huddersfield. West Yorks. HD2 1YF

**THIS BOOK SHOULD BE RETURNED ON OR BEFORE THE LATEST
DATE STAMPED BELOW. FINES ARE CHARGED AT THE RATE OF
10p PER WEEK OR ANY PART OF A WEEK BEYOND THIS DATE.**

ALMONDBURY 5/88
06 FEB 1989
LINTHWAITE
12|89

-7 JUN 1990
HONLEY
1|93
10.93

SKELMANTHORPE
11|99

780.91.

WATTERS
Its easy to play Children's Songs

You may renew this loan for a further period by post, telephone
or personal visit, provided that the book is not required by
another reader. Please quote the nine digit number above the
bar code label, and due date.

W72   NO MORE THAN THREE RENEWALS ARE PERMITTED.

250 039 530

Exclusive Distributors:
Music Sales Limited
78 Newman Street, London W1P 3LA, England
Music Sales Pty. Limited
27 Clarendon Street, Artarmon, Sydney, NSW 2064, Australia

This book © copyright 1981 by
Wise Publications
ISBN 0.86001.960.8
Order No. AM 29489

Art Direction by Mike Bell
Cover illustration by Paul Sample
Compilation by Peter Evans
Arranged by Cyril Watters

Music Sales complete catalogue lists thousands
of titles and is free from your local music
book shop, or direct from Music Sales Limited.
Please send 25p in stamps for postage to
Music Sales Limited, 78 Newman Street, London W1P 3LA.

Unauthorised reproduction of any part
of this publication by any means including photocopying
is an infringement of copyright.

Printed in England by
Eyre & Spottiswoode Ltd, Thanet Press
Margate, Kent

Sailing

Words & Music by Gavin Sutherland

© Copyright 1972 by Island Music Ltd, 22 St Peter's Square, London, W6.
All Rights Reserved. International Copyright Secured.

dark night far a-way._____ I am dy-ing,_____ for-ev-er try-ing, to be

C   G   A7   Em

with you, who can say._____ Can you | hear me, can you hear me, Thro' the
                                      sail-ing, we are sail - ing; Home a-

Am7   G   no chord   G   Em

dark night, far a - way._____ I am dy - ing, for-ev-er try-ing, to be
gain,_____ 'cross the sea._____ We are sail-ing,_____ stor-my wa - ters, to be

C   G   A7   Em

1   **2**

with you, who can say.   We are | free._____
near you, to be

Am7   G   D7   G

mp   *rallentando*

The Jimmy Brown Song
(The Three Bells)

English lyric by Bert Reisfeld
Music by Jean Villard (Gilles)

© Copyright 1945 Les Nouvelles Editions Meridian, Paris, France.
© Copyright 1948 Southern Music Publishing Co. Inc., New York, USA.
Southern Music Publishing Co. Ltd, 8 Denmark Street, London WC2.
All Rights Reserved. International Copyright Secured.

CHORUS *(with more movement)*

All the cha-pel bells were ring - ing in the lit - tle val-ley town,
All the cha-pel bells were ring - ing, t'was a great day in his life,
Just a lone-ly bell was ring - ing in the lit - tle val-ley town,

no chord   C   G

And the song that they were sing - ing was for ba - by Jim-my Brown.
'Cause the song that they were sing - ing was for Jim-my and his wife.
T'was fare-well that it was sing - ing to our good old Jim-my Brown.

G7   C

Then the lit - tle con-gre - ga - tion prayed for guid-ance from a - bove,
Then the lit - tle con-gre - ga - tion prayed for guid-ance from a - bove,
And the lit - tle con-gre - ga - tion prayed for guid-ance from a - bove,

E7   Am

"Lead us not in-to temp - ta-tion, bless this hour of med-i - ta-tion, guide him with e-ter-nal
"Lead us not in-to temp - ta-tion, bless oh Lord this cel-e - bra-tion, may their lives be filled with
"Lead us not in-to temp - ta-tion, may his soul find the sal - va-tion of Thy great e-ter-nal

Dm7   C   G7

1-2

love." ___
love." ___

2. There's a
3. From a

C

3

love." ___

C

7

Banks Of The Ohio

Traditional

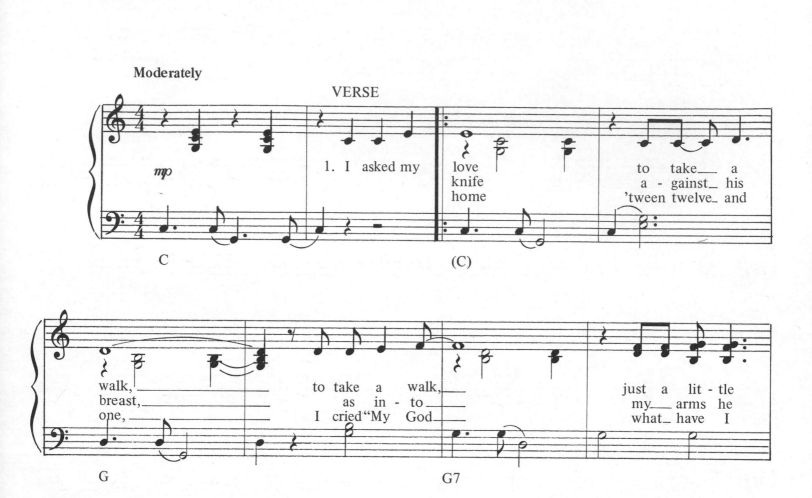

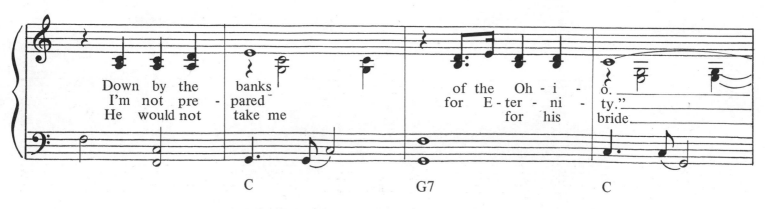

© Copyright 1981 Dorsey Brothers Music Limited London W1.
All Rights Reserved. International Copyright Secured.

CHORUS

And on - ly say   that you'll be   mine,

(C)   G

In no oth - er's arms en - twine.

G7   C

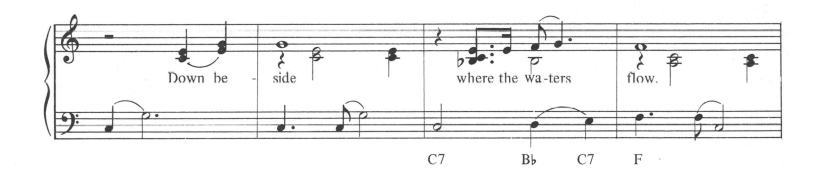

Down be - side   where the wa - ters   flow.

C7   B♭   C7   F

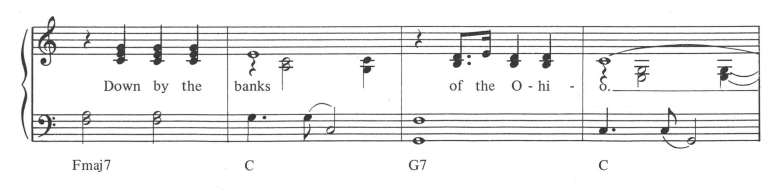

Down by the   banks   of the O - hi - o.

Fmaj7   C   G7   C

2. I held a
3. I wand-ered   Down by the   banks   of the Oh - i - o.

F   C   G7   C

9

Both Sides Now

Words & Music by Joni Mitchell

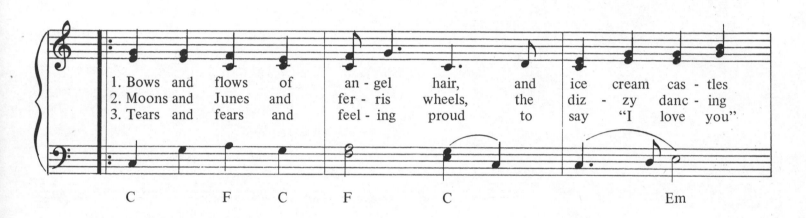

1. Bows and flows of an - gel hair, and ice cream cas - tles
2. Moons and Junes and fer - ris wheels, the diz - zy danc - ing
3. Tears and fears and feel - ing proud to say "I love you"

in the air,_____ and fea - ther can - yons ev - 'ry - where:_____
way you feel,_____ as ev - 'ry fai - ry tale comes real:_____
right out loud,_____ dreams__ and schemes and cir - cus crowds:_____

___ I've looked at clouds that way._____ But now they on - ly
___ I've looked at love that way._____ But now it's just a -
___ I've looked at life that way._____ But now old friends are

© Copyright 1967 Siquomb Publishing Corp, USA.
Westminster Music Ltd., 19/20 Poland Street, London W.1.

This Ole House

Words & Music by Stuart Hamblen

© Copyright 1954 Stuart Hamblen Music Co, USA.
Leeds Music Ltd, 138 Piccadilly, London W1
for the British Commonwealth (exc. Canada) and South Africa.
All Rights Reserved. International Copyright Secured.

trem - bles in the dark - ness when the light - nin' walks a - bout.
seeks a new to - mor - row through a gol - den win - dow pane. } Ain't a-gon-na

C7   F

need this house no long - er, ain't a-gon-na need this house no more. Ain't got

Bb   F

time to fix the shin - gles, ain't got time to fix the floor. Ain't got

C7   F

time to oil the hing - es nor to mend no win - dow panes. Ain't gon - na

Bb   F

need this house no long - er; He's a get-ting rea - dy to meet his fate. 2.3. This ole fate.

C7   F   F

De Do Do Do, De Da Da Da

Words & Music by Sting

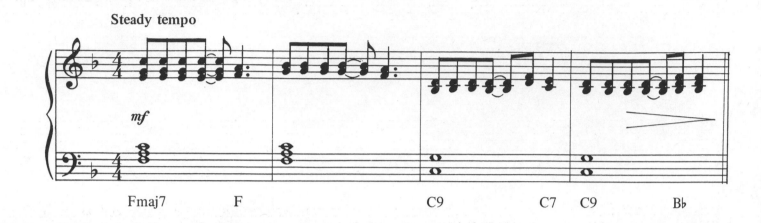

© Copyright 1980 Virgin Music (Publishers) Ltd,
2-4 Vernon Yard, Portobello Road, London W11.
All Rights Reserved. International Copyright Secured.

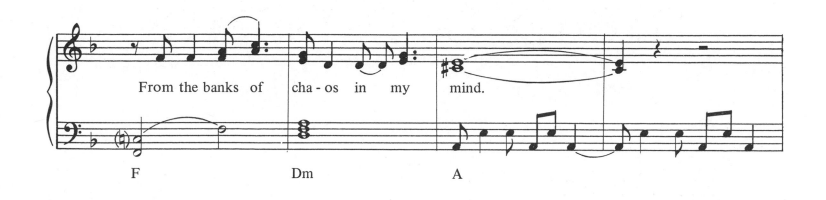

From the banks of cha-os in my mind.

F   Dm   A

And when their el-o-quence es-capes___ me,

Bb   C

Their lo-gic ties me up and rapes me.   De

Bb   C   Bb

do do do,   de da da da   is all I want___ to

F   C   F6

say to you,___   de do do do,   de da da da,   {their the

Bb   F

To Interlude

1
in - no - cence___ will / pull me through.___ De
mean-ing less___ and

C   F6   B♭

2
all that's true.___

F   B♭

3   *FINE*

all that's true.___

F   B♭   F

INTERLUDE

mp

G   E♭   F   C   G   E♭

F6   E♭   F6   E♭   F6   E♭   F6   E♭

D.S. al Fine

C9   B♭

(Do) The Hucklebuck

Words by Roy Alfred
Music by Andy Gibson

Steady rock tempo

no chord   G9   C7   Now

VERSE

here's   a dance you   should   know   Hey! Ba-by

F   B♭   Am   Gm   F   F7

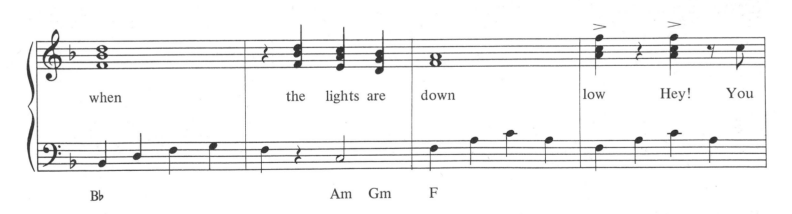

when   the lights are   down   low   Hey!   You

B♭   Am   Gm   F

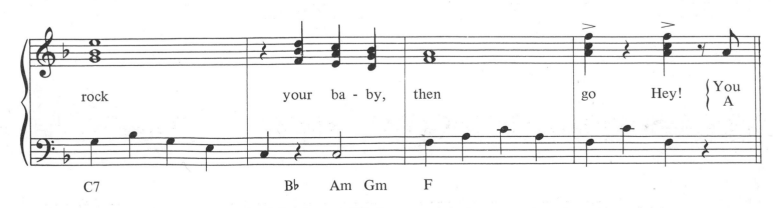

rock   your ba-by, then   go   Hey! { You
                                                          A

C7   B♭   Am   Gm   F

© Copyright 1949 United Music Corp., New York, USA.
Leeds Music Ltd, 138 Piccadilly, London W1
for the British Commonwealth (exc. Canada), Eire, South Africa and Europe.
All Rights Reserved. International Copyright Secured.

CHORUS

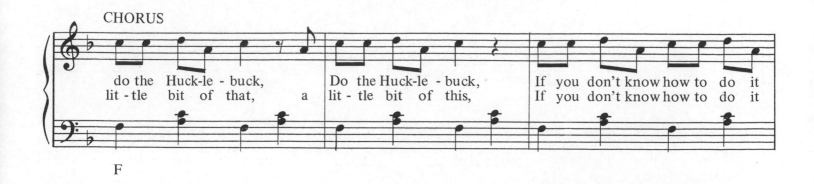

do the Huck-le - buck,　Do the Huck-le - buck,　If you don't know how to do it

lit - tle bit of that,　a lit - tle bit of this,　If you don't know how to do it

F

then you're out of luck.

ask my lit - tle sis.　Shove your Ba - by in,　twist her all a - round;

F7　　　　　　　　　　Bb

Then you start a - twist - ing it and mov-in' all a - round.　You wrig-gle like a snake,

F　　　　　　　　　　　　　　　　　　C7

1-2

wad-dle like a duck,　That's what you do when you do the Huck-le - buck. Now

Bb7　　　　　　　　F

3

do the Huck-le - buck.　A lit - tle bit of that,　a lit - tle bit of this

F

If you don't know how to do it ask my lit - tle sis. Shove your Ba - by in,

F7

Bb

twist her all a - round; Then you start a - twist-ing it and mov-in' all a - round. You

F

wrig-gle like a snake, wad-dle like a duck, That's what you do when you

C7

Bb7

F

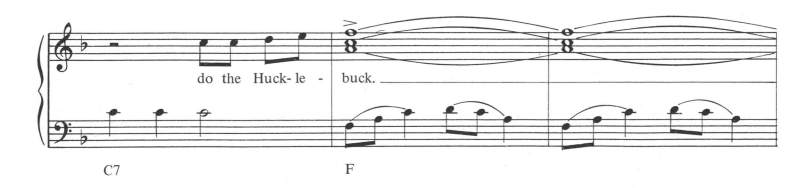

do the Huck-le - buck.

C7

F

Hey!

A Walk In The Park

Words & Music by Nick Bailey

Fairly slow

A walk in the park

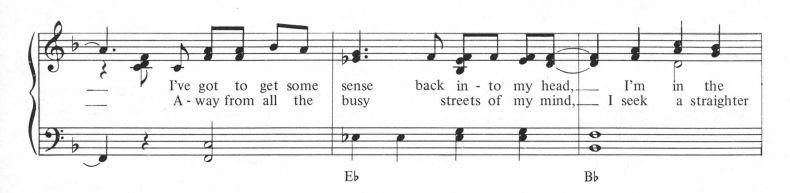

I've got to get some sense back in - to my head, I'm in the
A - way from all the busy streets of my mind, I seek a straighter

dark and I can't see where I'm bein' led.
path, I seek a shady glade in which to unwind,

I'd give the world to set the clock back and
but why do we go on, in spite of mis - takes, in

© Copyright 1979 Lynton Muir Music,
Electron House, Cray Avenue, Orpington, Kent for the World.
All Rights Reserved. International Copyright Secured.

act like a man.___ Where can I turn ___ to save my-self ___ from
spite of des-truc-tion,. life can be fun, ___ de- pend-ing on ___ your

Dm   Eb   Bb

CHORUS

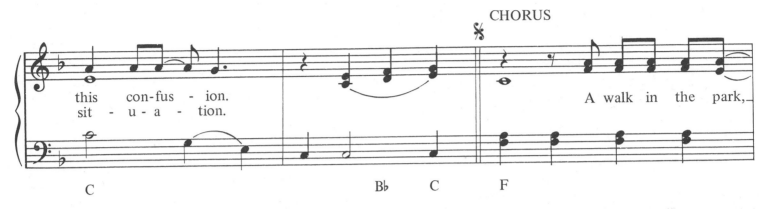

this con-fus - ion.   A walk in the park,___
sit - u -a - tion.

C   Bb   C   F

_ a step in the dark,_   A walk in the park,.

Am7   Bb   F

_ A trip in the dark,___   I'm get-ting a -

Am7   Bb   Dm

1   **2** *Repeat Chorus*
                                      for Fade

way, es-cap-ing to - day. ___   A walk in the park,.

F6   Ebmaj7   Bb   Bb

The Bucket Of Water Song

Words & Music by John Gorman

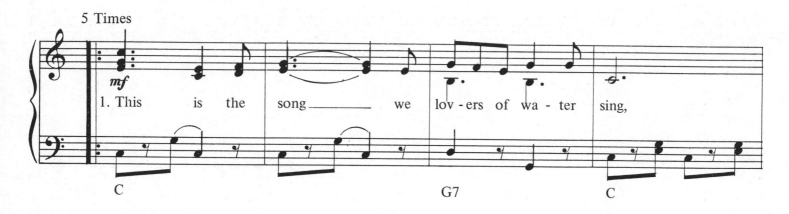

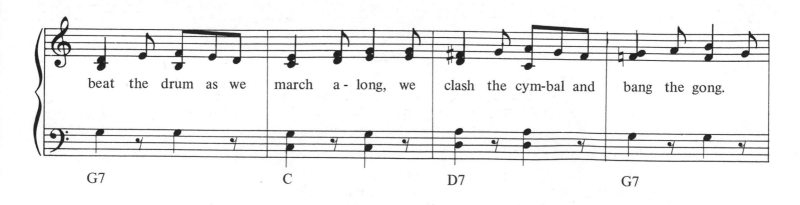

© Copyright 1980 PVA Music, Alpha Tower, ATV Centre, Birmingham.
All Rights Reserved. International Copyright Secured.

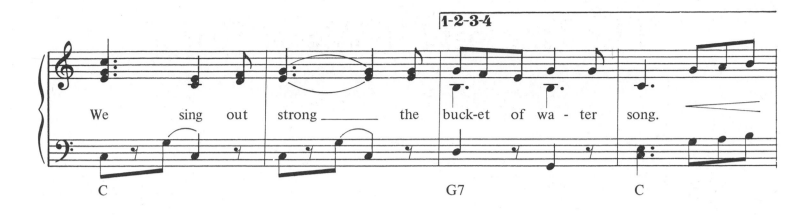

We sing out strong ____ the buck-et of wa - ter song.

C   G7   C

no chord   E7   A7   D7   G7

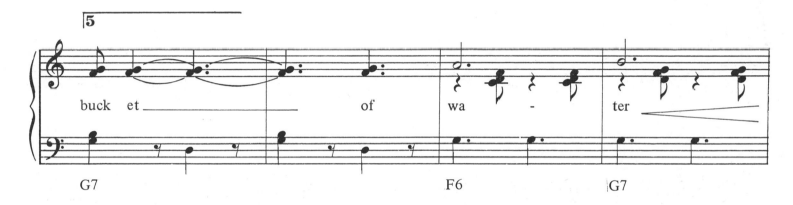

buck et _____ of   wa -   ter

G7   F6   G7

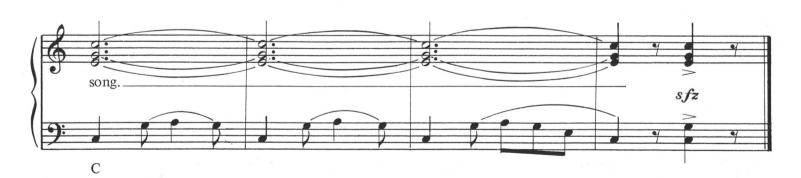

song. _____

C

Verse 2:   Stand on one leg and point up at the sun.
              Grab hold of your nose, we're sure it must be fun.
              But no matter who or what you are we know something you'll enjoy by far
              To sing out the song, the bucket of water song.

Verse 3/5:   *as Verse 1*

Verse 4:   Though life is hard we do the best we can.
(Spoken)   Against evil we guard to help our fellow man.
              We put the baddies in their place, we fight the foes of the human race,
              But whatever the case, we take it in the face.

Have Yourself
A Merry Little Christmas

Words & Music by Hugh Martin & Ralph Blane

When the stee-ple bells sound their "A", They don't play it in tune.

But the wel-kin will ring one day And that day will be soon.

Have your-self a mer-ry lit-tle Christ-mas, let your heart be light,

© Copyright 1944 & 1958 by Leo Feist Inc USA.
Administered by Big Three Music Ltd,
37/41 Mortimer Street, London, W1 for the UK & Eire.
All Rights Reserved. International Copyright Secured.

Some day soon we all will be to - ge - ther, if the fates al -

C   Dm7   G7   C

low,   Un - til then, we'll   have to mud - dle through some -

Dm7   G7   C   Dm7   E7

how;   So have your - self a mer - ry lit - tle Christ-mas

Am   C7   C7+   F   Am7   Dm7   G7 G7♭9

1

now.

C   F6   G7

2

now.

C   G7   C   G7

rallentando

C   F6   C

Shaddap You Face

Words & Music by Joe Dolce

Moderately

mp

(Spoken) "Hello, I'm a Guiseppe — I got something special for you. Ready? Uno Due Tre Quatro"

F

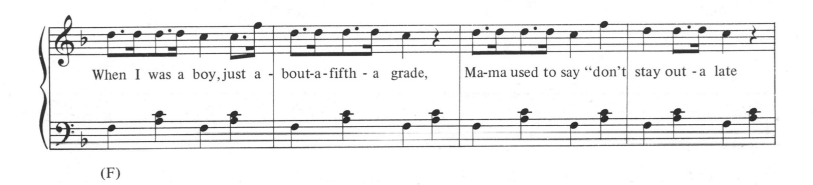

(F)

When I was a boy, just a - bout-a-fifth - a grade, Ma-ma used to say "don't stay out - a late

C7

with the bad - a boys, al - ways shoot the pool, Gui-sep - pe, don't funk-a school."

F

Bb7   F

Boy, it make - a me sick all the things I got - ta do, I
soon there come a day gon - na be a big - a star; then they

© Copyright 1980 April Music Ltd, 37 Soho Square, London W1.
All Rights Reserved. International Copyright Secured.

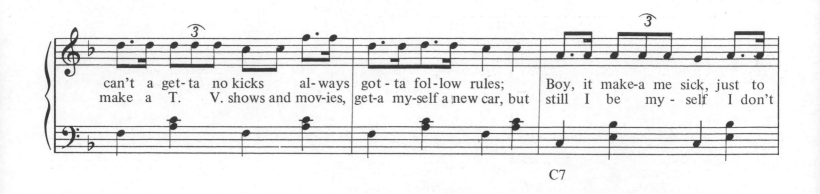

can't a get-ta no kicks al-ways got-ta fol-low rules; Boy, it make-a me sick, just to
make a T. V. shows and mov-ies, get-a my-self a new car, but still I be my - self I don't

C7

make a lou-sy bucks, got - ta feel - a like a fool. Spoken: and the Momma
want to change a thing, still - a dance____ and - a sing. used to say all the time:

F   Bb7

What's a mat-ter you, hey got - ta no res-pect, what-a you think you do, why you look-a so sad?

F

It's - a not so bad it's - a nice - a place, Ah shad-dap-a you face. (Spoken)
That's what

C7   F

my Momma can remem-ber.

28   Bb7   Fdim   C   C7   F   Fm

But -dap-a you face. (Spoken) Mama — she said it all the time.

Bb7   F   Bb7

(1,4,5,6) What's a mat-ter you, hey, got-ta no res-pect, what-a you think you do,
(2) As patter A (below)
(3) As patter B (below)

F

why you look-a so sad? It's-a not so bad, it's a nice-a place, Ah shad-

C7

dap-a you face.   dap-a you face.

F   Bb7   F

Patter A

Hello everybody
Out there in Radio and T.V. land
Did you know I had a big hit song in Italy
         with this
"Shaddap you face"
I sing this song and all my fans applaud
They clap their hands
That makes me feel so good.

Patter B

You ought to learn this song, it's real simple
I sing "What's a matter you"
You sing "Hey"
And I sing the rest and at the end we can
         all sing
"Shaddap you face"
Uno . . . Due . . . Tre . . . Quatro

(To Chorus)

Rivers Of Babylon

Words & Music by Farian, Reyam, Dowe and McMaughton

Moderately

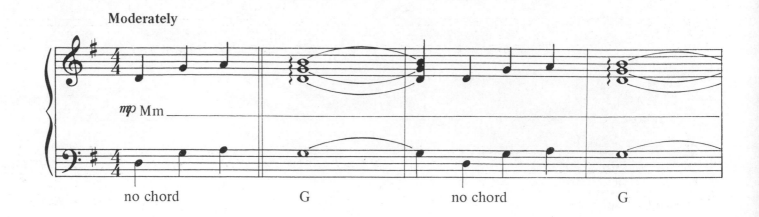

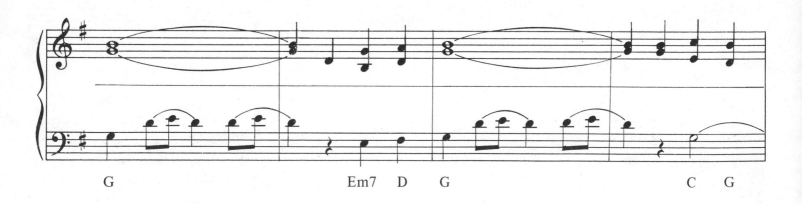

© Copyright Far Musikverlag & Beverlys Records for the world.
© Copyright 1978 Far Musikverlag/Hansa Productions/ATV Music Ltd/Blue Mountain Music Ltd
for the UK & Eire.
All Rights Reserved. International Copyright Secured.

To Coda ⊕

there we sat down, Yeah__ we wept

D7 G C G D

1 **2** *D.%. al Coda*

when we re-membered Zi - on. By the ri-vers of Ah _____

D7 C G Em7 D7 Em7 D7

CODA

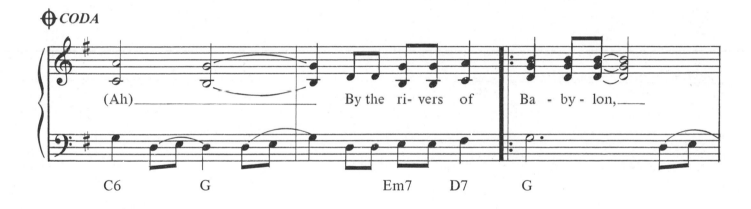

(Ah)_____ By the ri-vers of Ba - by-lon,___

C6 G Em7 D7 G

there we sat down, Yeah__ we wept

D7 G C G D

Repeat for Fade

when we re-mem-bered Zi - on. By the ri-vers of

D7 C G Em7 D7

I Believe In Father Christmas

Words by Peter Sinfield
Music by Greg Lake

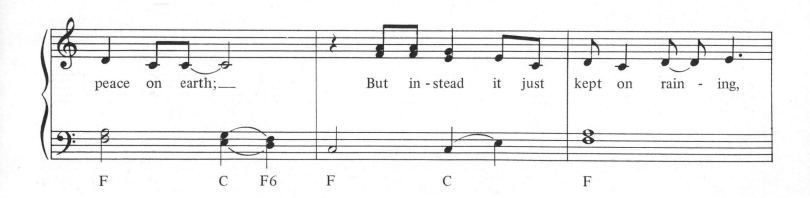

© Copyright 1975 MANTICORE MUSIC LTD, 3rd Floor, 71 Baker Street, London W1.
All Rights Reserved. International Copyright Secured.

Christ-mas morn-ing, A win-ter's light___ and a dis-tant choir,___ And the

C   Bb   F   C

peal of a bell and that Christ-mas tree smell, And their eyes full of tin-sel and fire.___

Cmaj7   C   F

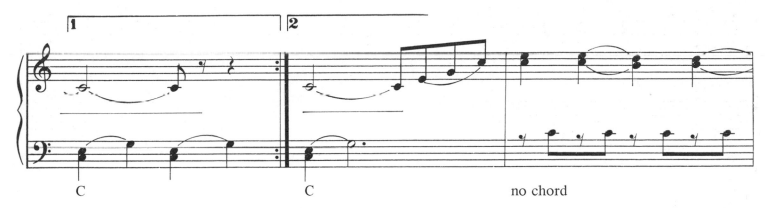

C   C   no chord

C

Verse 2:   They sold me a dream of Christmas,
They sold me a silent night;
And they told me a fairy story
Till I believed in the Israelite.
And I believed in Father Christmas,
And I looked to the sky with excited eyes,
Till I woke with a yawn in the first light of dawn
And I saw him and through his disguise.

Clair

Words & Music by Raymond O'Sullivan

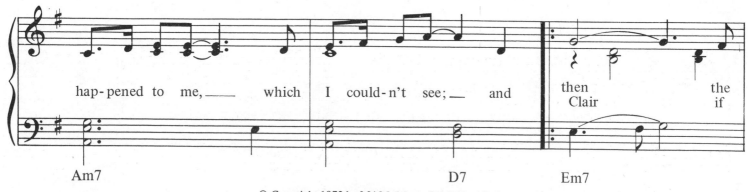

© Copyright 1972 by MAM (Music Publishing) Ltd,
24/25 New Bond Street, London, W1 for the world.
All Rights Reserved. International Copyright Secured.

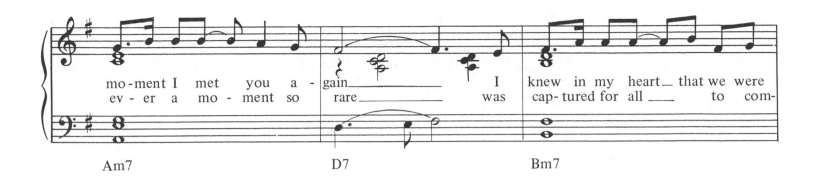

mo-ment I met you a-gain____ I knew in my heart__ that we were
ev-er a mo-ment so rare____ was cap-tured for all ___ to com-

Am7   D7   Bm7

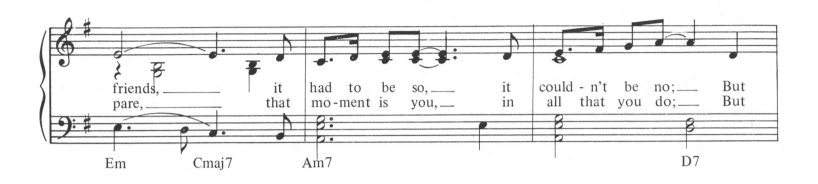

friends,_____ it had to be so,___ it could-n't be no;___ But
pare,_____ that mo-ment is you,__ in all that you do;___ But

Em   Cmaj7   Am7   D7

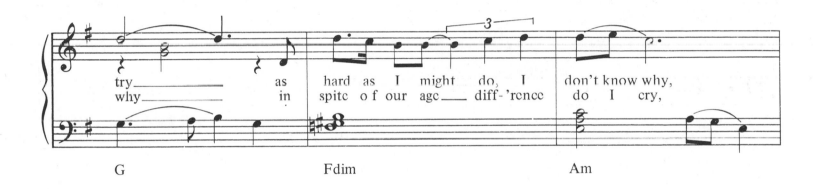

try_____ as hard as I might do, I don't know why,
why_____ in spite of our age__ diff-'rence do I cry,

G   Fdim   Am

You get to me__ in a way I can't de-scribe, Words mean so lit - tle when you
Each time I leave__ you I feel I could die, No - thing means more__ to me than

D7   G   C

look up and smile___ I don't care what peo-ple say____ to me, you're
hear - ing you say___ I'm going to mar - ry you, will____ you mar - ry

Am7   G

more than a child oh Clair, Clair._____
me, Un-cle Ray oh Clair, Clair._____

A7 **Am7** **Cmaj7** **D9**

Clair I've told you___ be-fore don't you dare get

Em7 **Am7** **D7** **C**

back in-to bed,___ can't you see that it's late,___ no you

G **Em7** **Am7** **D7**

can't have a drink,___ Oh al - right, then but wait___ just a

G **Em7** **Am7** **D7**

bit._____ While I in an ef - fort to ba - by sit,

G **Fdim** **Am**

Cap - ture my breath___ what there is left of it.

D7　　　　　　　　　　　　　　　G

You can be mur - der at this hour of the day,___ but in the

C　　　　　　　　　　　　　　Am7

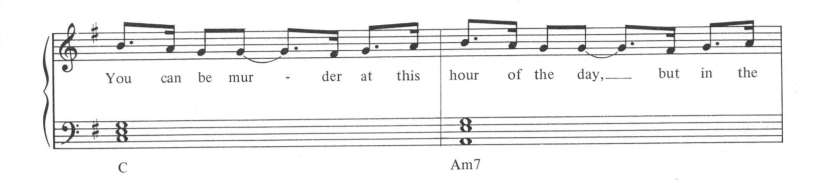

morn - ing, to - night___ will seem a life - time a - way.___ Oh

G　　　　　　　　　　　　　　A7

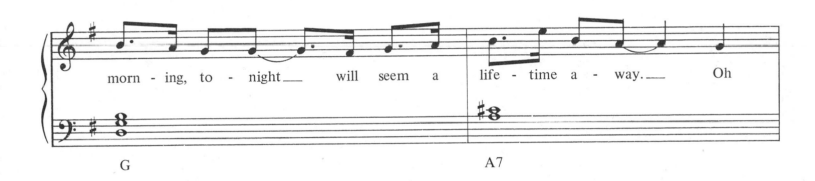

Clair,　　　　　　Clair,_____　　Clair. _____

Am7　　　　　　Cmaj7　　D9　　　G　　　Em7

A7　　　D7　　　　　G

Does Your Mother Know

Words & Music by Benny Andersson & Bjorn Ulvaeus

© Copyright 1979 for the world by Union Songs AB, Stockholm, Sweden.
Bocu Music Ltd, 48 Grafton Way, London, W1 for Great Britain and Eire.
All Rights Reserved. International Copyright Secured.

There's that look___ in your eyes,___
You're so cute,___ I like your style,___

G   Em

I can read___ in your face that your feel-ings are driv-ing you wild,___
And I know___ what you mean when you give me a flash of that smile,___

G   C   G   Am   G

Ah, but girl, you're on-ly a child.
Ah, but girl, you're on-ly a child.

D   D9   G

CHORUS

Well, I could dance with you, hon-ey, if you think it's fun-ny,

C   F   C   F

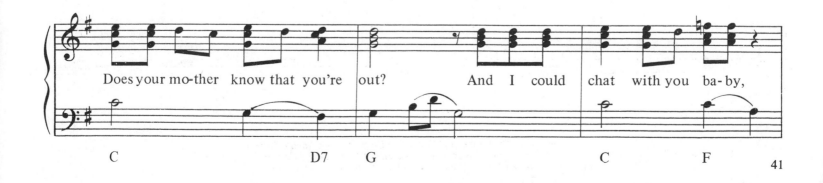

Does your mo-ther know that you're out? And I could chat with you ba-by,

C   D7   G   C   F

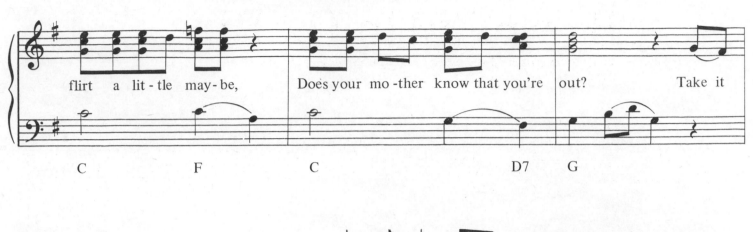

flirt a lit-tle may-be, Does your mo-ther know that you're out? Take it

C   F   C   D7   G

ea-sy,   bet-ter slow down, girl,___ that's no way to go.___ Does your

C   Cm   G   Cm

mo-ther know?___ Take it ea-sy,   try to cool it girl,___ play it

G   Cm   G   C   Cm

1   **2**

nice and slow.___ Does your mo-ther know?___   mo-ther know?___

G   Cm   G   Cm   G

C   Cm   G

Brown Girl In The Ring

Words & Music by Frank Farian & Stefan Klinkhammer

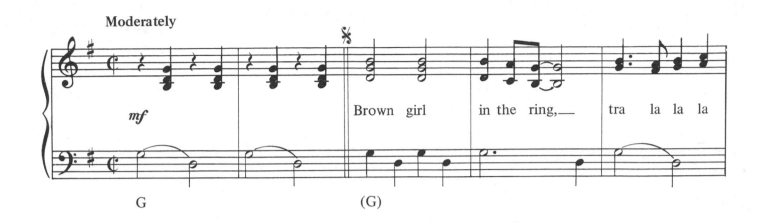

© Copyright 1978 Far Musikverlag GmbH for the World.
© Copyright 1978 Far Musikverlag/Hansa Productions Ltd/ATV Music Ltd,
24 Bruton Street, London W1 for the UK and Eire.
All Rights Reserved. International Copyright Secured.

tra la la la la, Come on show me a mo - tion, tra la

D

la la la la. Show me a mo - tion, tra la la la la, She

G

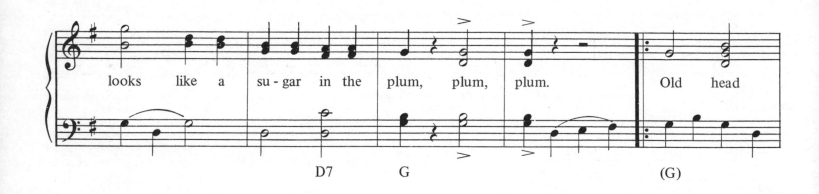

looks like a su - gar in the plum, plum, plum.   Old head

D7   G   (G)

wa - ter run dry,   no-where to wash my

D7

To Coda ⊕

|1| |2|

clothes. ___   I re - mem - ber one ___ Sat - ur - day ___

G

44

Amazing Grace

Traditional

Key 1st, 4th, 5th, 57
F   F Bb C C7
D   D G   A A7
G

Fairly slow

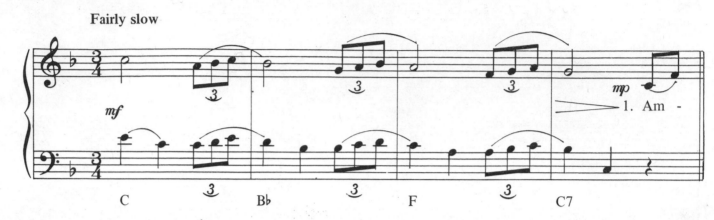

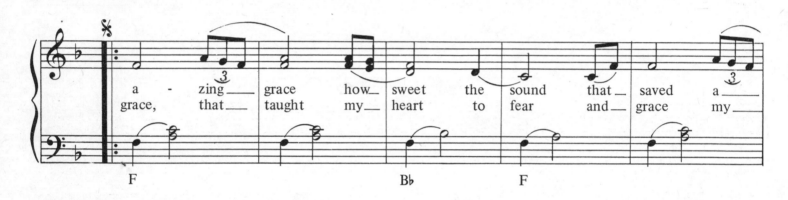

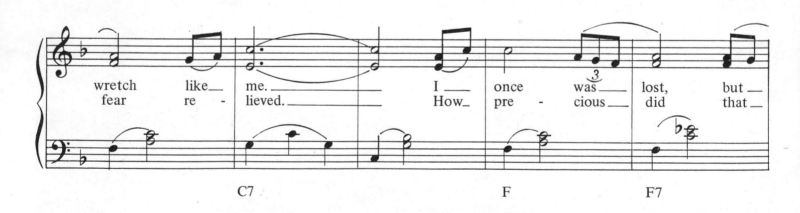

© Copyright 1981 Dorsey Brothers Music Limited, London W1.
All Rights Reserved. International Copyright Secured.